Get By on Your Own in German

A Situational Vocabulary

Jane Berlinka B.A. (Lond.)
Head of Modern Languages, Creighton School

and José Berlinka

Edward Arnold

© Jane Berlinka and José Berlinka 1981

First published 1981 by
Edward Arnold (Publishers) Ltd
41 Bedford Square, London WC1B 3DQ

British Library Cataloguing in Publication Data

Berlinka, Jane
    Get by on your own in German.
    1. German language — Glossaries, vocabularies etc.
    I. Title   II. Berlinka, José
    433'.2'1

    ISBN 0-7131-0526-7

Typeset in 8/9pt Century by
The Castlefield Press of Northampton,
and printed in Great Britain by
Belmont Press Ltd, Northampton.

Contents

Introduction

This book aims to be of practical use to visitors in German speaking countries.

It is designed to help tourists express themselves as well as understand what they might hear or see. In addition, teachers will find it useful when preparing their students for school journeys, oral examinations and dialogue writing.

Since most users of this book are likely to have a basic knowledge of German, elementary concepts such as numbers, days of the week etc. have not been included except where they arise in context. Words which are likely to be read rather than actively used by the tourist are usually listed at the beginning of each section. Many expressions would have a logical place in more than one topic area, but for the sake of brevity and economy they have not been repeated. Translations are strictly contextual, except in the alphabetical vocabularies where important alternative meanings are given.

The choice of lexical items has been determined by situational, not grammatical considerations. Thus the polite *and* familiar forms have been included only in situations where either one might arise. However, for the sake of the linguistically more enterprising, genders and plurals of nouns as well as principal parts of strong verbs are listed in the German—English alphabetical vocabulary and genders of nouns are included in the English—German alphabetical vocabulary.

1

Coping with language problems

Ich verstehe nicht.	I don't understand.
Sprechen Sie (sprichst du) Englisch/Französisch?	Do you speak English/French?
Könnten Sie (könntest du) für mich übersetzen, bitte?	Could you translate for me, please?
Sprechen Sie (sprich) bitte langsamer!	Please speak more slowly!
Wie heißt das auf Deutsch?	What do you call this in German?
Was bedeutet das?	What does this mean?
Wie schreibt man das?	How do you write this?
Wie buchstabiert man das?	How do you spell this?
Würden Sie (würdest du) das wiederholen, bitte?	Would you repeat this, please?
Sie sprechen (du sprichst) zu schnell!	You speak too fast!
Haben Sie (hast du) ein Wörterbuch?	Have you got a dictionary?
Wie sagt man auf Deutsch . . . ?	How do you say in German . . . ?
Verstehen Sie (verstehst du), was ich meine?	Do you understand (know) what I mean?

2

Basic courtesies

danke	thank you (thanks)
danke schön } danke vielmals	thank you very much / thanks a lot
vielen Dank	many thanks
herzlichen Dank	my heartiest thanks
Ich bedanke mich	I thank you
guten Morgen	good morning
guten Tag	good day (for saying 'hallo' only)
guten Abend	good evening
gute Nacht	good night
auf Wiedersehen	good bye (see you again, see you soon, etc.)
tschüß	cheerio, ta-ta, bye-bye
viel Vergnügen } viel Spaß	have fun

Ich bin Ihnen (dir) sehr dankbar.	I am very grateful to you.
bitte	please
bitte schön } bitte sehr }	you are welcome don't mention it that's quite all right }

In German, any expression of thanks is always followed by the standard acknowledgement of: *bitte, bitte schön, bitte sehr* or even *bitte bitte*.

Entschuldigen Sie! (Entschuldige!)	Excuse me!
Verzeihung!	Pardon — Pardon me! I beg your pardon!
Das (es) tut mir leid.	I am sorry.
Machen Sie sich (mach dir) bitte keine Mühe!	Don't go to any trouble, please!
Bitte, nach Ihnen!	After you, please.

3
Travel

By Rail

(Haupt) Bahnhof	(main) station
Fahrkarten	tickets
Gepäckaufbewahrung	left luggage
Toiletten	toilets
Herren	gents
Damen	ladies
Auskunft	information
Reisebüro	travel office
(Platz) Reservierungen	(seat) reservations
Gaststätte	restaurant
Schnellimbiß	snack bar
Warteraum	waiting room
Fernsprecher	telephones
Ankunft	arrival
Abfahrt	departure
Bekanntmachung	announcement
zu den Zügen	to the trains
Bahnsteigkarten	platform tickets
Gleis	platform
Gepäckträger	porter
T E (Trans Europa)	Trans-European (Express)
D-Zug	fast train

Eilzug	fast train with various stops
Personenzug	slow train (stopping at every station)
einmal München	one ticket to Munich
einfach	single
zweite Klasse	2nd class
zweimal Köln	two tickets to Cologne
hin- und zurück	return
erste Klasse	1st class
mit Zuschlag	with supplement (extra charge)
ohne Zuschlag	without supplement
Wann geht der nächste Zug nach Hameln?	When is the next train to Hamelin?
Von welchem Gleis geht er?	From which platform does it leave?
Muß ich umsteigen?	Do I have to change?
Ist das der Zug nach Nürnberg?	Is this the train for Nuremberg?
Um wieviel Uhr komme ich in Hannover an?	At what time do I arrive in Hanover?
Wann kommt der Zug aus Frankfurt an?	When does the train arrive from Frankfurt?
Auf welchem Gleis?	On which platform?
Hat der Zug Verspätung?	Is the train late?
Ist der Zug pünktlich?	Is the train on time?
Habe ich Anschluß in Dortmund?	Have I got a connection in Dortmund?

By Air

Flughafen	airport
Fluginformationstafel	flight information board
Inland-Flüge	domestic flights
Ausland-Flüge	European and overseas flights
Abfertigung	check-in
Abflug	(flight) departure
Verspätung	delay
erwartet um 15.30 Uhr	expected at 3.30 p.m.
gelandet	landed
Abflugshalle	departure lounge
Berlin — auf den Namen Hamilton gebucht!	Berlin — booked in the name of Hamilton.
Ich möchte meinen Flug bestätigen.	I should like to confirm my flight.

Ich möchte meine Flugkarte abholen.	I should like to collect my (air) ticket.
Ist das ein Lufthansa oder B A-Flug?	Is this a Lufthansa or a B A flight?
Ich habe bloß Handgepäck.	I only have hand luggage.
Habe ich Übergewicht?	Have I excess weight?

By Boat

Hafen	port (docks)
zu den Fähren	to the ferries
Hafenrundfahrten	harbour circuits (round trips)
kein Zutritt	no admission
kein Durchgang	no throughway
Ich möchte eine (Einzel) Kabine.	I should like a (single) cabin.
Haben sie noch Liegeplätze?	Have you still got some rest chairs?
Geht hier die Fähre nach Dänemark?	Does the ferry for Denmark go from here?

At Customs

Zoll	Customs
Paßkontrolle	passport control
Ist das Ihr Koffer?	Is this your suitcase?
Machen Sie mal auf!	Open it up!
Ich habe nichts zu verzollen.	I have nothing to declare.
Ich habe ein paar Geschenke.	I have a few presents.
Zeigen Sie mal, bitte!	Show me, please!
Ich habe eine Flasche Wein.	I have a bottle of wine.
Ihren Paß, bitte!	Your passport, please!

Public Transport in Town

U-Bahn	underground train
S-Bahn (Schnellbahn)	urban railway
Straßenbahn	tram
Autobus	bus
Schnellbus	express bus
Fahrkartenautomat	ticket machine (automatic)
Fahrkartenentwertung	slot for inserting ticket to be stamped with date, time and fare stage
vorn/hinten einsteigen	enter in front/at the back
nur Ausstieg	exit only
Behinderte	invalids, physically handicapped
Einstieg nur mit gültigem Fahrschein/Fahrausweis	no admission without valid ticket

4

hier drücken	press here (for doors to open)
nächste Haltestelle	next stop (press button if you wish to alight)
zurücktreten, bitte!	step back, please.

4
Motoring

At a Garage

Tankstelle	petrol station
Tankwart	petrol pump attendant
Münzentankstelle	coin operated pump
Ölwechsel	oil change
Reifen	tyres
Batterien	batteries
Frostschutz	anti-freeze
Autozubehör	car accessories
Windschutzscheiben ersetzt	windscreens replaced
vollautomatische Waschstraße	fully automatic car-wash
Reparaturen	repairs
Super	four star petrol
Normal	three star petrol
Selbstbedienung	self service
außer Betrieb	out of order

Voll auftanken, bitte!	Fill her up, please!
Super oder Normal?	four star or three star?
Dreißig Liter Normal!	thirty litres of three star!
Eine Flasche destilliertes Wasser, bitte!	A bottle of distilled water, please.
Prüfen Sie bitte	Please check
das Öl	the oil
das Wasser	the water
die Reifen	the tyres
die Batterie	the battery
Alles in Ordnung!	Everything's okay!
Sie brauchen einen halben Liter Öl!	You need half a litre of oil.

Car Problems

Mit meinem Wagen ist etwas nicht in Ordnung:	Something is wrong with my car:
der Vergaser	the carburettor
der Verteiler	the distributor
der Dynamo	the dynamo
die Zündkerzen	the spark plugs

5

der Kühler	the radiator
der Starter	the starter
die Zündung	the ignition
Er springt nicht an.	It won't start.
Er springt schlecht an.	It starts badly.
Er zieht nicht.	It is sluggish, doesn't pull.
die Bremsen	the brakes
die Fußbremse	the foot brake
die Handbremse	the hand brake
der Öldruck	the oil pressure
die Benzinpumpe	the fuel pump
die Wasserpumpe	the water pump
der Ventilator	the fan
der Ventilatorriemen	the fan belt
Die Batterie lädt nicht auf.	The battery doesn't charge.
Die Batterie ist leer.	The battery is flat.
die Schaltung	the gears
der Schalthebel	the gear lever
erster/zweiter/dritter/ vierter Gang	1st/2nd/3rd/ 4th gear
der Rückwärtsgang	reverse gear
das Getriebe	the gearbox
die Kupplung	the clutch
Die Heizung funktioniert nicht!	The heating doesn't work!
die Scheibenwischer	the windscreen wipers
Ich habe einen Platten.	I have a flat tyre.
das Vorderrad	the front wheel
das Hinterrad	the back wheel
das Ersatzrad	the spare wheel
der Ersatzreifen	the spare tyre
Der Druck ist zu hoch!	The pressure is too high!
zu wenig Druck	not enough pressure
die Steuerung	the steering
das Steuerrad	the steering wheel
die Blinklichter	the indicators (winkers)
die Lampen	the headlamps
die Scheinwerfer	the headlights
Ich brauche eine neue Birne.	I need a new bulb.
das Rückfahrtslicht	the reversing light
die Nebellampe	the fog light
das Bremslicht	the brake light
die Hecklampen	the rear lights
die Hupe	the horn
die Sicherheitsgürtel	the safety belts

Car Breakdown

Haben Sie einen Wagenheber?	Have you got a jack?
Könnten Sie mich abschleppen, bitte?	Could you tow me, please?
Könnten Sie mich ein Stück anschieben?	Could you push me a bit?
Würden Sie die Autohilfe/ Polizei anrufen?	Would you call the breakdown service/police?

5

Money matters

ein Pfennig	a Pfennig
zwanzig Pfennig	twenty Pfennigs
ein Groschen	a ten Pfennig coin (popular expression)
ein Fünfzigpfennigstück	a fifty Pfennig coin
eine Mark	one Mark
ein Zweimarkstück	a two Mark coin
zehn Mark	ten Marks
ein Zwanzigmarkschein	a twenty Mark note
drei Mark fünfzig	three Marks fifty
Bank	bank
Wechselstube	change (office for changing currency)
Wechsel	change (counter for changing currency in a bank)

Ich möchte englische Pfund umwechseln!	I should like to change English Pounds.
Wieviele?	How many?
Fünfzig Pfund	fifty Pounds
Wie steht der Kurs?	What is the rate of exchange?
Vier Mark elf zum Pfund	four Marks eleven to the Pound
Ich möchte einen Reisescheck einlösen	I should like to cash a traveller's cheque.
Haben Sie Ihren Reisepaß hier?	Have you got your passport with you?
Unterschreiben Sie, bitte!	Sign, please.
Gehen Sie zur Kasse, bitte!	Go to the paying-out counter, please.
Wieviel ist das in englischem Geld?	How much is this in English money?
Was kostet das?	How much does it cost?
Ich habe noch genug Geld	I have enough money

7

nicht mehr viel Geld	not much money left
kein Geld mehr	no more money
Ich bin pleite!	I am broke!
Das kann ich mir nicht leisten!	I can't afford that!
Das ist mir zu teuer!	That's too expensive for me!
Das ist sehr preiswert.	That's good value for money.
Das ist billig!	That's cheap!
Ich habe kein Kleingeld.	I have no small change.
Könnten Sie mir einen Hundertmarkschein wechseln?	Could you change a hundred Mark note?

6

Finding your way in town

Wo ist . . . ?	Where is . . . ?
der Marktplatz	the market square
der Tiergarten	the zoo
die Jugendherberge	the youth hostel
die Kathedrale ⎫ der Dom ⎬	the cathedral
das Münster	the Minster
die Polizeiwache	the police station
das Einkaufszentrum	the shopping centre
das Rathaus	the town hall

Gibt es in diesem Ort hier	Is there . . . in this place?
eine evangelische/ katholische Kirche	a Protestant/ Catholic church
ein Museum	a museum
ein Theater	a theatre
ein Kino	a cinema
eine Sportanlage	a sports centre
ein Freibad	an open air swimming pool
ein Hallenbad	an indoor swimming pool
eine (Kunst) Eisbahn	an ice rink
eine Diskothek	a discotheque
eine Zimmervermittlung ⎫ einen Zimmernachweis ⎬	an accommodation bureau

Ist das weit?	Is it far?
Nein, das ist ganz in der Nähe.	No, it's very near.
etwa dreihundert Meter	about 300 metres
gleich um die Ecke	just round the corner
etwa fünf Minuten zu Fuß	about five minutes' walk

eine gute halbe Stunde	a good half hour
Am besten nehmen Sie die Straßenbahn.	You had better go by tram.

Wo ist . . .	Where is the nearest . . .
der nächste Briefkasten	letter box
der nächste Supermarkt	supermarket
die nächste Apotheke	chemist's
die nächste Bäckerei	bakery
die nächste Fleischerei	butcher's shop
die nächste Buchhandlung	bookshop
die nächste Post	Post Office
die nächste Straßenbahn (Bus)-Haltestelle	tram (bus) stop
das nächste Blumengeschäft	florist's
das nächste Café	café

Wie komme ich am besten . . .	Which is the best way to . . .
zum Konrad Adenauer-Platz	Konrad Adenauer Square
zur Bismarck-Straße	Bismarck Street
zur Stadtmitte	the town centre
Sie müssen links/rechts abbiegen.	You have to turn left/right.
Sie gehen am besten geradeaus.	You'd best go straight ahead.
dann die erste links	then the first on the left
die zweite rechts	the second on the right
bis zur Ampel	as far as the traffic light
bis zur Kreuzung	as far as the junction
Überqueren Sie . . .	Cross at the . . .
beim Fußgängerstreifen	pedestrian crossing
bei der Unterführung	subway
dann ist es auf der rechten/ linken Seite	then it's on the right/left hand side
Fährt diese Straßenbahn (dieser Bus) zum Schloß?	Does this tram (bus) go to the castle?
Ja, ganz richtig.	Yes, that's right.
Nein, da brauchen Sie die Nummer fünfzehn.	No, you need a number 15.

7

Finding accommodation

At an Hotel or Guest-House

Zimmer (zu vermieten)	rooms (to let)
Zimmer frei	vacancies (rooms free)

Hotel besetzt	hotel is full (no vacancies)
Pension	guesthouse
Hotelnachweis ⎫	
Hotelvermittlung ⎰	hotel guide
Empfang	reception
Speisesaal	dining room
Fahrstuhl	lift
Haben Sie . . .	Have you got . . .
ein Einzelzimmer	a single room
ein Doppelzimmer	a double room
ein Dreierzimmer	a room for three
mit Bad	with bath
mit Dusche	with a shower
mit Frühstück	with breakfast
mit Halbpension	with breakfast and one meal
mit Vollpension	with breakfast and two meals
Wir servieren nur Frühstück.	We only serve breakfast.
Wir servieren keine Mahlzeiten.	We don't serve meals.
Für wie lange?	For how long?
Für . . .	For . . .
eine Nacht	one night
zwei Nächte	two nights
eine Woche	one week
Ist der Preis inklusiv?	Is the price inclusive?
Ja, alles ist inbegriffen.	Yes, everything is included.
Möchten Sie sich das Zimmer ansehen?	Would you like to see the room?
Es ist auf der ersten/zweiten/ dritten Etage.	It is on the first/second/ third floor.
Tragen Sie sich hier ein, bitte!	Fill in the register, please!
Um wieviel Uhr kann man essen?	At what time can one eat?
Frühstück von sieben bis neun	breakfast from 7 a.m. to 9 a.m.
Mittagessen von zwölf bis vierzehn Uhr	lunch from 12 p.m. to to 2 p.m.
Abendessen ab achtzehn Uhr	dinner as from 6 p.m.
Hier ist Ihr Schlüssel.	Here is your key.
Wann schließt das Hotel nachts?	When does the hotel close at night?
Nach Mitternacht müssen Sie klingeln.	After midnight you have to ring the bell.

10

At a Camping Site

Campingplatz	camping site
Verwaltung	camp administration
Waschraum	wash room
Büro	office
Spielplatz	playground
Nahrungsmittel und Getränke	food and drink
Campingkocher	camping stoves
Holzkohle	charcoal
Boote zu vermieten	boats for hire

Gäste sind gebeten sich nach Ankunft im Büro zu melden.	Guests are requested to register at the office after arrival.
Bürozeiten	office hours
vormittage zwischen acht und zehn Uhr	between 8 a.m. and 10 a.m.
abends zwischen achtzehn und einundzwanzig Uhr	evenings between 6 p.m. and 9 p.m.

Haben Sie noch einen Platz?	Have you still got a place?
Zelt oder Wohnwagen?	Tent or caravan?
Der Platz kostet sieben Mark fünfzig pro Übernachtung.	The place costs seven Marks fifty per night.
Ihre Autonummer, bitte?	Your car registration, please.

At a Youth Hostel

Jugendherberge	youth hostel
Herbergsvater/ Herbergsmutter	warden
Schlafsaal	dormitory
Küche	kitchen
Aufenthaltsraum	lounge, day room
Anmeldung	reception

Ihren Ausweis, bitte!	Your papers, please.
Ihre Mitgliedskarte, bitte!	Your membership card, please.
Rauchen verboten!	no smoking.

8
Shopping

Geschäftszeiten	hours of business
geöffnet	open

täglich von acht bis achtzehn Uhr	daily from 8 a.m. to 6 p.m.
Sonnabend nachmittag geschlossen	Saturday afternoon closed
Wegen Umbau geschlossen	closed for renovation
Sommerschlußverkauf	summer sale

At a Stationer's/Newsagent's

Schreibwaren	writing materials
Spielwaren	toys
Spiele	games
Zeitungen	newspapers
Zeitschriften	magazines

Haben Sie:	Have you got:
Ansichtskarten	picture postcards
Landkarten	maps
Straßenkarten	road maps
einen Stadtplan	a town map
Kugelschreiber	ballpoint pens
englische Zeitungen	English newspapers
schwarz/weiß Filme	black and white films
Farbfilme	colour films
Ich möchte . . . kaufen	I should like to buy:
ein Andenken	a souvenir
eine kleine Puppe	a little doll
ein Spielzeug für einen Jungen	a toy for a boy
Briefpapier	writing paper
einen Briefblock und Umschläge	a writing pad and envelopes
einen Notizblock	a note pad
einen Skizzierblock	a sketchblock
Wieviel darf es kosten?	What price category were you thinking of?
Wir haben eine schöne Auswahl.	We have a good selection.
Welche Farbe?	What colour?
Ich nehme das hier	I'll take this one here.

At the Baker's

Bäckerei-Konditorei	bakery-confectioner's
fünf Brötchen, bitte!	five rolls, please!
ein Weißbrot	a loaf of white bread
ein Schwarzbrot	a loaf of brown bread
ein Kilo oder ein Pfund?	a kilo or a pound?
ein Eierzopf	a loaf of Viennese bread

12

eine Schwarzwäldertorte	a Black Forest gateau (a regional speciality containing rich, creamy chocolate)
eine Kirschtorte	a cherry-brandy gateau (a creamy cake, laced with *Kirsch*, a potent drink distilled from cherries)
vier Berliner Pfannkuchen	four doughnuts
drei Stück Schokoladekuchen	three pieces of chocolate cake
zwei Stück Käsekuchen	two pieces of cheesecake
ein Paket Kekse	a packet of biscuits
ein Paket Zwieback	a packet of rusks
ein Päckchen Knäckebrot	a packet of Swedish style crisp bread
Darf's sonst noch was sein?	Anything else?
Nein, das ist alles.	No, that's all.

At the Butcher's

Fleischwaren	meats
Wurstwaren	sausages
Fleischerei/Schlachterei/ Metzgerei	butcher shop (expression depends on region)
Sonderangebot	special offer
Heute ganz frisch	freshly made today
eine Bockwurst	a longish, thick sausage
zwei Knackwürste	two shortish, thick sausages
eine Thüringer Bratwurst	a long, thin frying sausage
eine Mettwurst	a Salami-type sausage
ein Kilo Siedfleisch	a kilo of stewing beef
ein Schweinebraten	a pork joint
ein Rindsbraten	a beef joint
ein Hammelbraten	a lamb joint
ein Schweins(Kalbs)schnitzel	a fillet of pork/veal
ein Steak	a steak
ein Schweinskotelett	a pork chop
drei Hammelkoteletts	three lamb chops
hundert Gramm Aufschnitt	100 grammes of sliced cold meat
zweihundertfünfzig Gramm (= ein halbes Pfund) Schinken/Frühstücksspeck	250 grammes (= half a pound) of ham/bacon
Fünfhundert Gramm (= ein Pfund) Hackfleisch	500 grammes (= a pound) of minced meat
Darf's etwas mehr sein?	All right if it's a bit over?
Nein, lieber etwas weniger.	No, I'd rather have a bit under.

13

9
At the Post Office

	signs above various counters
Postwertzeichen	Stamps
Paketannahme	Parcels
Einzahlungen	Paying-in counter
Telegramme	Telegrams
Ferngespräche	Telephone calls

eine Fünfzig-Pfennig-Marke	a fifty Pfennig stamp
zwei Sechzig-Pfennig-Marken	two sixty Pfennig stamps
vier Siebzig-Pfennig-Marken	four seventy Pfennig stamps
ein Luftpostbrief	an aerogramme

Was kostet:	How much is:
eine Postkarte	a post card
ein Brief	a letter
ein Eilbrief	an express letter
ein Einschreibebrief	a registered letter
nach England	to England

Ich möchte London anrufen.	I should like to ring London.
Welche Nummer?	What number?
Kabine vier	Booth number four
Ich möchte ein R-Gespräch nach London.	I should like to ring London collect (reverse the charges).
Ihren Namen, bitte!	Your name, please!
Das Gespräch ist angenommen.	Your call has been accepted.
Bitte sprechen!	Go ahead, please!
Das Gespräch ist verweigert.	Your call has been refused.
Die Gebühr ist eine Mark zwanzig.	The charge is one Mark twenty.
Nachzahlen, bitte!	Please insert more money. (This warning lights up in coin-operated telephone kiosks ten seconds before disconnection.)

10
Going to a restaurant or café

Gasthaus	restaurant
Gasthof	inn
Raststätte	motorway restaurant

Weinstube	wine bar
Für Garderobe wird nicht gehaftet.	No liability accepted for hats, coats, etc.
Speisekarte	menu
Weinkarte	wine list
Menu	menu (as opposed to *à la carte*)
Tagessuppe	soup of the day
Schweinebraten	roast pork
Hähnchen	chicken
Bratwurst	fried sausage
Erbsen	peas
Grüne Bohnen	french beans
Pommes Frites	French fried potatoes (chips)
Salat	salad
Apfelstrudel	applestrudel
Erdbeertorte mit Sahne	strawberry gateau with cream
Eis	ice cream
Bedienung und Mehrwertsteuer inbegriffen.	inclusive of service and V.A.T.
Möchten Sie essen?	Would you like to eat?
Wir nehmen das Menu.	We are taking the menu.
Viermal Tagessuppe.	Soup of the day for four.
Dreimal Schweinebraten mit Erbsen und Salat.	Roast pork with peas and salad for three.
Einmal Hähnchen mit Pommes Frites.	One chicken with chips.
Was trinken Sie . . .	What would you like to drink . . .
ein Bier/einen Sprudel/ einen Apfelsaft	a beer/mineral water/ apple juice
eine Kola	a Coke
eine Tasse Kaffee/Tee	a cup of coffee/tea
ein Glas Rotwein	a glass of red wine
einen Schoppen Weißwein	a 2cl jug of white wine
Was nehmen Sie zum Nachtisch?	What would you like for a sweet? (dessert)
Was für Eis haben Sie . . .	What kinds of ice cream have you got . . .
Vanille, Schokolade, Mokka	vanilla, chocolate, coffee
Herr Ober!	Waiter!
Fräulein	Miss! (Waitress!)
Zahlen bitte!	The bill, please.
Alles zusammen oder separat?	All together or separately?

11
Staying with a family

Meeting Your Hosts

Willkommen in Deutschland!	Welcome to Germany!
Es freut mich, Sie (dich) kennenzulernen.	I am pleased to meet you.
Sind Sie (bist du) gut gereist?	Did you have a good trip?
Sind Sie (bist du) sehr müde?	Are you very tired?
Es geht	Not too bad
Wie war die Überfahrt?	How was the crossing?
Das Meer war stürmisch/ ruhig.	The sea was stormy (rough)/ calm.
Wie lange hat die Reise gedauert?	How long did the trip take?
zehn Stunden	ten hours
Ich bin seit gestern nachmittag unterwegs.	I've been travelling since yesterday afternoon.
Ist das Ihr (dein) ganzes Gepäck?	Is this all your luggage?
Geben Sie (gib) mir Ihren (deinen) Koffer!	Give me your suitcase!
Unser Wagen steht gleich da vorn.	Our car is just out there.
Wir nehmen ein Taxi.	We'll take a taxi.

Asking for Things in the Home

Wo ist . . . ?	Where is . . . ?
das Badezimmer	the bathroom
der Mülleimer	the dustbin
der Lichtschalter	the light switch
die Steckdose	the wall plug (point)
der Aschenbecher	the ashtray
Darf ich . . . ?	May I . . . ?
baden	take a bath
duschen	take a shower
mein Hände/Haare waschen	wash my hands/hair
zu Bett gehen	go to bed
eine Schallplatte auflegen	play a record
fernsehen	watch television
Radio hören	listen to the radio
rauchen	smoke
meinen Freund/meine Freundin/meine Eltern anrufen	ring up my friend/girl friend/parents
nähen/waschen/bügeln	do a bit of sewing/washing/ ironing

16

Stört es Sie, wenn ich rauche?	Do you mind if I smoke?
Könnten Sie mir . . . geben?	Could you give me . . . ?
ein Handtuch	a towel
ein Badtuch	a bathtowel
einen Waschlappen	a flannel
Zahnpasta	toothpaste
Seife	a soap
einen Haartrockner (Föhn)	a hair dryer
eine Haar (Kleider)-bürste	a hair (clothes) brush
einen Kamm	a comb
ein Taschentuch	a handkerchief
etwas Tinte	some ink
eine Sicherheitsnadel	a safety pin
etwas Zwirn	some cotton (thread)
eine Nähnadel	a sewing needle
eine Schere	a pair of scissors
etwas Waschpulver	some washing powder
das Bügeleisen	the iron
einen Aschenbecher	an ashtray

At Table

Guten Appetit! Mahlzeit!	Enjoy your meal!
Mögen Sie (magst du) . . .	Do you like . . .
Saft	fruit juice
Kakao	cocoa
Pumpernickel	very dark rye bread
Honig	honey
ein weichgekochtes/	a soft-boiled/
hartgekochtes Ei	hard-boiled egg
Käse	cheese
Quark	cottage cheese
eine klare Brühe	consommé (clear soup)
Frikadellen	meat balls
Kabeljau	cod
Scholle	plaice
Wurzeln (Möhren)	carrots
Spinat	spinach
Rosenkohl	Brussels sprouts
Blumenkohl	cauliflower
Kartoffelpuffer	croquette potatoes
Kartoffelbrei	mashed potatoes
Tomaten	tomatoes
Rettich	radishes
(saure) Gurken	gherkins
Ja, das mag ich.	Yes, I like that.
Nein, danke, ich mag/	No, thank you, I don't like
vertrage das leider nicht.	that/unfortunately, it
	doesn't agree with me.

17

Versuchen Sie (versuch) das mal!	Come on, try it!
Schmeckt's?	Do you like it? (of food)
Das ist eine deutsche Spezialität.	That's a German speciality.
Darf ich Ihnen (dir) noch etwas geben/nachgießen?	May I give you/pour you a little more?
Das ist sehr lecker!	That's very tasty!
Das schmeckt prima!	That tastes wonderful!
Danke, ich habe genug!	Thank you, I've had enough.
Ich nehme gern noch einen Schluck ein wenig	I'll gladly have another drop a bit more
Nein, danke, ich bin nicht hungrig/durstig.	No, thank you, I am not hungry/thirsty.

Being Helpful

Kann ich Ihnen (dir) helfen ...	Can I help you ...
das Geschirr spülen	wash up
abtrocknen	dry the dishes
den Tisch decken	lay the table
abräumen	clear the table
Kann ich Ihnen etwas besorgen?	Can I do some shopping for you?

Showing Appreciation

Sie sind (du bist) sehr liebenswürdig.	You are very kind.
Sie haben sich (du hast dir) viel Mühe gemacht.	You have gone to a lot of trouble.
Ich bedanke mich herzlich.	I thank you very much.
Ich habe Ihnen (dir) eine Kleinigkeit mitgebracht.	I have brought you a little something.
Hier ist ein kleines Geschenk für Sie (für dich).	Here is a little present for you.
Ich habe mich bei Ihnen (bei dir) sehr wohlgefühlt.	I have felt very much at home here.
Ich hoffe, Sie (dich) bald wiederzusehen.	I hope to see you again soon.

12

Talking about yourself and your family

Wie heißen Sie (heißt du)?	What are you called?
Wie ist Ihr (dein) Name?	What is your name?
Wie heißt er/sie?	What is he/she called?

Ich heiße . . .	I'm called . . .
Mein Vorname/Familienname ist . . .	My first name (Christian name)/surname is . . .
Woher kommen Sie (kommst du)?	Where are you from?
Wo wohnen Sie (wohnst du)?	Where do you live?
Ich komme aus England/ Schottland/Wales/ Nordirland.	I am from England/Scotland/ Wales/Northern Ireland.
Ich wohne in . . .	I live in . . .
Wie alt sind Sie (bist du)?	How old are you?
Ich bin sechzehn.	I am sixteen.
Ich war im Januar fünfzehn.	I was fifteen in January.
Ich werde im Juli siebzehn.	I shall be seventeen in July.
Haben Sie (hast du) Geschwister?	Have you got brothers and sisters?
Ja, ich habe einen Bruder/ eine Schwester/zwei Brüder/zwei Schwestern.	Yes, I have a brother/ a sister/two brothers/ two sisters.
Ich bin ein Einzelkind.	I am an only child.
Was ist Ihr (dein) Vater/ Ihre (deine) Mutter von Beruf?	What is your father's/ mother's occupation?
Er ist . . .	He is a . . .
Kaufmann	businessman
Beamter	civil servant
Ingenieur	(an) engineer
Mechaniker	mechanic
Vertreter	representative
Lehrer	teacher
Lastfahrer	lorry driver
Rechtsanwalt	lawyer
Landwirt	farmer
Bergmann	miner
Musiker	musician
Bahnangestellter	railway employee
Seemann	sailor
Fabrikarbeiter	factory worker
Er hat sein eigenes Unternehmen.	He has his own business/ he is self-employed.
Sie ist . . .	She is a . . .
Lehrerin	teacher
Journalistin	journalist
Schriftstellerin	writer
Sekretärin	secretary
Krankenschwester	nurse
Kindergärtnerin	nursery teacher
Verkäuferin	saleslady

19

Arztgehilfin	medical assistant
Fürsorgerin	social worker
Hausfrau	housewife
Laborantin	laboratory assistant
kaufmännische Angestellte	clerk (office worker)
Kassiererin	cashier
Künstlerin	artist

13
Health problems

Mir ist nicht gut.	I don't feel well.
Mir ist . . .	I feel . . .
übel	sick
schwindlig	dizzy
Was ist denn los?	What's the matter?
Wo fehlt's denn?	What's wrong?
Ich habe . . .	I have . . .
Zahnschmerzen	a tooth-ache
Kopfschmerzen	a headache
Ohrenschmerzen	an ear-ache
Magenschmerzen	a stomach-ache
Rückenschmerzen	backache
Nasenbluten	a nose bleed
Husten	a cough
den Schnupfen	a cold
Grippe	the 'flu
Fieber	a temperature
Heuschnupfen	hayfever
einen Ausschlag	a rash
Ich habe . . .	I have . . .
mir den Fuß verstaucht	sprained my foot
mich geschnitten	cut myself
eine Schwellung hier	a swelling here
Ich bin allergisch dagegen.	I am allergic to it.
Es tut mir weh hier.	I've got a pain here.
Es ist geschwollen.	It is swollen.
Haben Sie (hast du) . . .	Have you got . . .
ein Fieberthermometer	a thermometer
Aspirin	aspirins
Pflaster	sticky plaster
ein Desinfektionsmittel	a disinfectant
Verbandstoff	a dressing
Salbe	any ointment
Hustenbonbons	coughsweets (lozenges)

20

Damenbinden	sanitary towels
Haben Sie (hast du) etwas gegen . . .	Have you got something something for . . .
Schmerzen	pains
Verdauungsbeschwerden	indigestion
Durchfall	diarrhoea
Verstopfung	constipation
Kater	a hangover

Ich muß . . .	I must . . .
zum Arzt	see a doctor
zum Zahnarzt	see a dentist
ins Krankenhaus	go to hospital
zur Apotheke	go to a chemist's shop
Könnten Sie für mich einen Termin vereinbaren?	Could you make an appointment for me?

Wie geht es Ihnen (dir) jetzt?	How are you now?
Wie fühlen Sie sich (fühlst du dich) jetzt?	How do you feel now?
Es geht mir	I feel . . .
gut	fine
besser	better
nicht sehr gut	unwell
schlechter	worse
gute Besserung	get well soon

14
Losing personal belongings

Ich habe meinen Reisepaß verloren.	I have lost my passport.
Gibt es hier ein Britisches Konsulat?	Is there a British Consulate here?
Man hat mir meine Fahrkarte, mein Geld, etc. gestohlen.	Someone has stolen my ticket, money, etc.
Gehen Sie doch zur Polizei!	You'd better go to the police!

Fundbüro	lost property office
Ich habe . . . verloren.	I have lost . . .
meine Fahrkarte	my ticket
mein Geld	my money
meine Reiseschecks	my traveller's cheques
mein Portemonnaie	my purse
meine Brieftasche	my wallet
meine Handtasche	my handbag
meinen Schlüssel	my key

21

meinen Fotoapparat	my camera
meinen Regenmatel/Schirm	my raincoat/umbrella
meine Windjacke	my anorak
meine Jacke	my jacket (cardigan)
meine Handschuhe	my gloves
meine Armbanduhr	my wrist-watch
meinen Ring	my ring
meine Ohrringe	my earrings
mein Armband	my bracelet
meine Halskette	my pendant (necklace)
meine Manschettenknöpfe	my cuff links

Ich habe leider nichts gefunden!	I didn't find anything, unfortunately!
Fragen Sie (Frag) mal im Fundbüro!	Enquire at the Lost Property Office!

Wo } haben Sie diesen Wann } Artikel verloren?	Where } did you lose When } this item?
In der Straßenbahn Nummer sieben.	On a number seven tram.
Im Autobus Nummer zwölf.	On a number twelve bus.
Ich bin nicht sicher.	I am not sure.
Ich glaube bei einem Kiosk in der Gustav Mahler-Straße.	I think near a kiosk on Gustav Mahler Street.
Heute vormittag/nachmittag.	This morning/afternoon.
Gestern/vorgestern.	Yesterday/the day before yesterday.
Gestern abend.	Yesterday evening.

Beschreiben Sie den Artikel!	Describe the item.
Er ist aus	It's made of:
Leder	leather
Plastik	plastic
Gold	gold
Silber	silver
Er ist	It is
rot	red
grün	green
braun	brown
schwarz	black
gelb	yellow
blau	blue
weiß	white
Welche Marke?	What make?
Wie hoch schätzen Sie den Wert?	How much do you think it's worth?
Schwer zu sagen . . .	Difficult to say . . .
Mindestens fünfzig Mark.	At least fifty Marks.

22

Ungefähr hundert Mark.	About a hundred Marks.
Er ist nicht sehr wertvoll.	It isn't very valuable.
Er hat nur sentimentalen Wert.	It's only of sentimental value.
Ihr Name und Ihre Anschrift, bitte!	Your name and address, please.
Kommen Sie in ein paar Tagen wieder vorbei!	Call back in a few days.

Vocabulary

German — English

German	English
ab	as from
abbiegen (biegt . . . ab, bog . . . ab, ist abgebogen)	to turn off
das Abendessen (-)	dinner, evening meal
abends	in the evening
die Abfahrt (-en)	departure
die Abfertigung (-en)	check-in
der Abflug (¨e)	flight departure
die Abflugshalle (-n)	departure lounge
abholen (holt . . . ab)	to collect, meet
abschleppen (schleppt . . . ab)	to tow (away)
abtrocknen (trocknet . . . ab)	to dry the dishes
allergisch	allergic
alles	everything
alles in Ordnung	everything's okay
alt	old
am besten	best
die Ampel (-n)	traffic light
das Andenken (-)	souvenir
ankommen (kommt . . . an, kam . . . an, ist angekommen)	to arrive
die Ankunft (¨e)	arrival
die Anmeldung (-en)	reception, registration
annehmen (nimmt . . . an, nahm . . . an, hat angenommen)	to accept
anrufen (ruft . . . an, rief . . . an, hat angerufen)	to ring up
anschieben (schiebt . . . an, schob . . . an, hat angeschoben)	to give a push
der Anschluß	connection
die Anschrift (-en)	address
ansehen (sieht . . . an, sah . . . an, hat angesehen)	to look at, to view
die Ansichtskarte (-n)	picture postcard
anspringen (springt . . . an, sprang . . . an, ist angesprungen)	to start (of car)
der Apfelsaft	apple juice
der Apfelstrudel (-)	apple strudel

24

die Apotheke (-n)	chemist's shop
das Armband (¨er)	bracelet
die Armbanduhr (-en)	wrist-watch
der Artikel (-)	article, item
der Arzt (¨e)	doctor
die Arztgehilfin (-nen)	medical assistant (fem.)
der Aschenbecher (-)	ashtray
das Aspirin (-s)	aspirin
auf	on
auf Deutsch	in German
auf Wiedersehen	good bye (see you again etc.)
der Aufenthaltsraum (¨e)	lounge, day room
aufladen (lädt . . . auf, lud . . . auf, ist aufgeladen)	to (re)charge (of battery)
aufmachen (macht . . . auf,)	to open up
der Aufschnitt	sliced cold meat
auftanken (tankt . . . auf,)	to tank up, fill up
aus	out of, from, made of
außer Betrieb	out of order
die Auskunft (¨e)	information
der Ausland-Flug (¨e)	European or overseas flight
der Ausschlag (¨e)	rash
die Auswahl (-en)	choice
der Ausweis (-e)	documentary evidence, official paper, credential
der Autobus (se)	bus
die Autohilfe (-n)	breakdown service
die Autonummer (-n)	car registration
der Autozubehör	car accessories
die Bäckerei (-en)	bakery
das Bad (¨er)	bath
baden	to bathe
das Badtuch (¨er)	bathtowel
das Badezimmer (-)	bathroom
der Bahnangestellte (-n)	railway employee
der Bahnhof (¨e)	station
die Bahnsteigkarte (-n)	platform ticket
bald	soon
die Bank (-en)	bank, bench
die Batterie (-n)	battery
der Beamte (-n)	civil servant, official
(sich) bedanken	to thank
bedeuten	to mean
die Bedienung	service, tip
Behinderte	invalids

bei	at
die Bekanntmachung (-en)	announcement
die Benzinpumpe (-n)	fuel pump, petrol pump
der Bergmann (¨er)	miner
der Berliner Pfannkuchen (-)	doughnut
der Beruf (-e)	profession, job, occupation
beschreiben (beschreibt, beschrieb, hat beschrieben)	to describe
besser	better
bestätigen	to confirm
das Bett (-en)	bed
das Bier	beer
billig	cheap
die Birne (-n)	(light) bulb, pear
bis	until
bitte	please
bitte schön } bitte sehr }	you're welcome, don't mention it
blau	blue
das Blinklicht (-er)	indicator, winker
bloß	only
das Blumengeschäft (-e)	florist's
der Blumenkohl	cauliflower
die Bohne (-n)	bean
die Bratwurst (¨e)	frying sausage
brauchen	to need
braun	brown
die Bremse (-n)	brake
das Bremslicht (-er)	brakelight
der Brief (-e)	letter
der Briefblock (¨e)	writing pad
der Briefkasten (¨)	letter box
das Briefpapier	writing paper
die Brieftasche (-n)	wallet
britisch	British
das Brot (-e)	bread
das Brötchen (-)	roll
der Bruder (¨-)	brother
buchen	to book
die Buchhandlung (-en)	bookshop
buchstabieren	to spell
bügeln	to iron
das Bügeleisen (-)	iron
das Büro (-s)	office
die Bürozeiten (pl.)	office hours
das Café	café
der Campingofen (¨-)	camping stove

der Campingplatz (¨e)	camping site
dagegen	against it
die Dame (-n)	lady
die Damenbinde (-n)	sanitary towel
dankbar sein	to be grateful
danke	thank you (thanks)
danke schön }	thanks a lot, thank you
danke vielmals }	very much
darf ich	may I
darf's etwas mehr sein	All right if it's a bit over
darf's sonst noch was sein	anything else
das kann ich mir nicht leisten	I can't afford that
das tut mir leid	I am sorry
dauern	to last, take (of time)
da vorn	in front there, out there
das Desinfektionsmittel (-)	disinfectant
destilliert	distilled
deutsch	German
Deutschland	Germany
dieser/e/es	this
die Diskothek (-en)	discotheque
der Dom (-e)	cathedral
das Doppelzimmer (-)	double room
dreimal	three times
das Dreierzimmer (-)	a room for three
(der/die/das) dritte	third
der Druck	pressure
der Durchfall	diarrhoea
der Durchgang (¨e)	throughway
durstig	thirsty
die Dusche (-n)	shower
duschen	to take a shower
der D-Zug (¨e)	fast train
die Ecke (-n)	corner
das Ei (-er)	egg
der Eierzopf (¨e)	Viennese bread
eigen	own
der Eilbrief (-e)	express letter
der Eilzug (¨e)	fast train (with various stops)
einfach	single (ticket)
das Einkaufszentrum (-en)	shopping centre
einlösen (löst . . . ein)	to cash (a cheque)
einmal	once, for one
einmal München	one ticket to Munich
ein paar	a few
der Einschreibebrief (-e)	registered letter

Einstieg nur mit gültigem Fahrschein	no admission without valid ticket
(sich) eintragen (trägt sich . . . ein, trug sich . . . ein, hat sich eingetragen)	to fill in (a register)
ein wenig	a little
die Einzahlung (-en)	paying-in counter
die Einzelkabine (-n)	single cabin
das Einzelkind (-er)	only child
das Eis	ice, ice cream
die Eltern (pl.)	parents
der Empfang (¨e)	reception
englisch	English
entschuldigen	to excuse
die Erbse (-n)	pea
die Erdbeertorte (-n)	strawberry gateau
das Ersatzrad (¨er)	spare wheel
der Ersatzreifen (-)	spare tyre
ersetzen	to replace
(der/die/das) erste	first
erste Klasse	first class
erwarten	to expect
es geht	not too bad, alright
es geht mir gut	I feel fine
es gibt	there is, there are
es freut mich	I am pleased
essen (ißt, aß, hat gegessen)	to eat
die Etage (-n)	floor, storey
etwa	about, approximately
etwas besorgen	to get something, do some shopping
etwas	something
etwas weniger	a little less, a bit under
evangelisch	Protestant
der Fabrikarbeiter (-)	factory worker
die Fähre (-n)	ferry
die Fahrkarte (-n)	ticket
der Fahrkartenautomat (-en)	ticket machine
die Fahrkartenentwertung	slot for inserting ticket for stamping
der Fahrstuhl (¨e)	lift
der Familienname (-n)	surname
der Farbfilm (-e)	colour film
die Farbe (-n)	colour
das Ferngespräch (-e)	telephone call
fernsehen (sieht . . . fern, sah . . . fern,	to watch television

hat ferngesehen)

der Fernsprecher (-)	telephone
das Fieberthermometer (-)	thermometer
der Film (-e)	film
finden (findet, fand, hat gefunden)	to find
die Flasche (-n)	bottle
die Fleischerei (-en)	butcher's shop
die Fleischwaren (pl.)	meats
der Flug (¨e)	flight
der Flughafen (¨)	airport
die Fluginformationstafel (-n)	flight information board
die Flugkarte (-n)	flight ticket, air ticket
der Föhn (-e)	hairdryer
der Fotoapparat (-e)	camera
fragen	to ask
französisch	French
das Fräulein (-s)	Miss, waitress
frei	free, vacant
das Freibad (¨er)	open air swimming pool
der Freund (-e)	friend (masc.)
die Freundin (-nen)	friend (fem.)
die Frikadelle (-n)	meat ball
frisch	fresh
der Frostschutz	anti-freeze
das Frühstück	breakfast
der Frühstücksspeck	bacon (for grilling)
(sich) fühlen	to feel
das Fundbüro (-s)	lost property office
funktionieren	to function, to work
für	for
für Garderobe wird nicht gehaftet	no liability accepted for hats, coats, etc.
für mich	for me
die Fürsorgerin (-nen)	social worker (fem.)
der Fuß (¨ße)	foot
(zu) Fuß	on foot
die Fußbremse (-n)	footbrake
der Fußgängerstreifen (-)	pedestrian crossing
der (erste, zweite, dritte, vierte) Gang	(first, second, third, fourth) gear
ganz (adj.)	whole
ganz in der Nähe	very near by
ganz richtig	that's right, quite right
der Gast (¨e)	guest
das Gasthaus (¨er)	restaurant
der Gasthof (¨e)	inn

die Gaststätte (-n)	restaurant
geben (gibt, gab, hat gegeben)	to give
gebeten	requested
die Gebühr (-en)	charge, fee
gehen (geht, ging, ist gegangen)	to go
gelandet	landed
gelb	yellow
das Geld	money
genug	enough
geöffnet	open
das Gepäck	luggage
die Gepäckaufbewahrung	left luggage
der Gepäckträger (-)	porter
geradeaus	straight ahead
die Geschäftszeiten (pl.)	hours of business
das Geschenk (-e)	present
das Geschirr	crockery, dishes
das Geschirr spülen	to do the washing up
geschlossen	closed
die Geschwister (pl.)	brothers and sisters
geschwollen	swollen
das Gespräch (-e)	conversation, call
gestern	yesterday
gestern abend	yesterday evening
das Getränk (-e)	drink
das Glas (¨er)	glass
glauben	to believe, think
gleich um die Ecke	just round the corner
das Gleis (-e)	platform
das Gold	gold
das Gramm (-e)	gramme
die Grippe	'flu
der Groschen (-)	10-Pfennig coin (popular expression)
grün	green
die Gurke (-n)	cucumber
gut	good, well
guten Appetit	enjoy your meal
guten Abend	good evening
guten Morgen	good morning
gute Nacht	good night
guten Tag	good day
gute Besserung	get well soon
das Haar (-e)	hair
die Haarbürste (-n)	hairbrush
der Haartrockner (-)	hairdryer
haben (hat, hatte, hat gehabt)	to have

das Hackfleisch	minced meat
der Hafen (-)	port, harbour
die Hafenrundfahrt (-en)	harbour circuit (round trip)
das Hähnchen (-)	chicken
halb	half
die Halbpension (-en)	breakfast and one meal
das Hallenbad (¨er)	indoor swimming pool
die Halskette (-n)	necklace, pendant
die Haltestelle (-n)	(tram or bus) stop
der Hammelbraten	lamb joint
die Hand (¨e)	hand
die Handbremse (-n)	handbrake
der Handschuh (-e)	glove
die Handtasche (-n)	handbag
das Handtuch (¨er)	towel
hart gesotten	hard-boiled
der Hauptbahnhof (¨e)	main station
die Hausfrau (-en)	housewife
die Hecklampe (-n)	rear light
heißen (heißt, hieß, hat geheißen)	to call (something), to be called
die Heizung (-en)	heating
helfen (hilft, half, hat geholfen)	to help
der Herr (-en)	gentleman (gents)
herzlich	heartily
herzlichen Dank	my heartiest thanks
der Heuschnupfen (-)	hayfever
heute	today
hier	here
hier drücken	press here (for doors to open)
hin und zurück	return (ticket)
hinten einsteigen	enter at the back
das Hinterrad (¨er)	back wheel
hoch	high
hoffen	to hope
die Holzkohle (-n)	charcoal
der Honig	honey
hören	to hear
das Hotel (-s)	hotel
der Hotelnachweis ⎱ die Hotelvermittlung ⎰	hotel guide
der Hundertmarkschein	hundred Mark note
hungrig	hungry
die Hupe (-n)	horn, hooter
der Husten	cough
das Hustenbonbon (-s)	cough sweet

ich möchte	I would like
ich vertrage das leider nicht	that doesn't agree with me
in	in
inbegriffen	included
der Ingenieur (-e)	engineer
inklusiv	inclusive
der Inland-Flug (⁝e)	domestic flight
die Jacke (-n)	jacket
jetzt	now
die Journalistin (-nen)	journalist
die Jugendherberge	youth hostel
der Junge (-n)	boy
der Kabeljau	cod
die Kabine (-n)	cabin, booth
der Kaffee	coffee
der Kakao	cocoa
der Kamm (⁝e)	comb
der Kartoffelpuffer (-)	croquette potato
der Kartoffelbrei	mashed potatoes
der Käse	cheese
der Käsekuchen (-n)	cheese cake
die Kasse (-n)	till, cash desk, paying out counter
die Kassiererin (-nen)	cashier (fem.)
der Kater	hangover
die Kathedrale (-n)	cathedral
katholisch	Catholic
der/die kaufmännische Angestellte (-n)	clerk, office worker
kein (-e)	no, not a
der Keks (-e)	biscuit
kennenlernen (lernt ... kennen)	to meet, become acquainted
das Kilo	Kilo
die Kindergärtnerin (-nen)	nursery teacher (fem.)
der Kiosk (-e)	kiosk
die Kirschtorte (-n)	cherry-brandy gateau
die klare Brühe	consommé, clear soup
die Kleiderbürste (-n)	clothes brush
klein	small
die Kleinigkeit (-en)	a little something, trifle
klingeln	to ring (a bell)
das Knäckebrot (-e)	crisp bread
der Koffer (-)	suitcase
die Kola (-s)	Coke (Coca Cola)
die Konditorei (-en)	confectioner's, cake shop

das Konsulat (-e)	consulate
die Kopfschmerzen (pl.)	headache
das Kotelett (-s)	(meat) chop
das Krankenhaus (¨er)	hospital
die Krankenschwester (-n)	nurse
die Kreuzung (-en)	junction
die Küche (-n)	kitchen
der Kugelschreiber (-)	ball point pen
der Kühler (-)	radiator (of cars)
die Künstlerin (-nen)	artist (fem.)
der Kurs (currency)	rate of exchange
die Laborantin (-nen)	laboratory assistant (fem.)
die Lampe (-n)	lamp
landen	to land
die Landkarte (-n)	map
der Landwirt (-e)	farmer
langsamer	more slowly
der Lastfahrer (-)	lorry driver
lecker	tasty
das Leder	leather
leer	empty, flat (of battery)
der Lehrer (-), die Lehrerin (-nen)	teacher
leider	unfortunately
der Lichtschalter (-)	light switch
liebenswürdig	kind
lieber	rather
der Liegeplatz (¨e)	rest chair
links	left
der Liter (-)	litre
der Luftpostbrief (-e)	aerogramme, air letter
machen	to make, do
machen Sie sich (mach dir) keine Mühe	don't go to any trouble
die Magenschmerzen (pl.)	stomach-ache
die Mahlzeit (-en)	meal
Mahlzeit!	enjoy your meal
der Manschettenknopf (¨e)	cuff link
die Mark	Deutsch-Mark
die Marke (-n)	make, (postage) stamp
der Marktplatz (¨e)	market square
der Mechaniker (-)	mechanic
das Meer (-e)	sea
mehr	more
die Mehrwertsteuer (-n)	V.A.T.
(sich) melden	to register

33

der Meter (-)	metre
die Metzgerei (-en)	butcher's shop
mindestens	at least
die Minute (-n)	minute
mir ist nicht gut	I don't feel well
mir ist schwindlig	I feel dizzy
mir ist übel	I feel sick
mit	with
mitbringen (bringt . . . mit, brachte . . . mit, hat mitgebracht)	to bring along
die Mitgliedskarte	membership card
das Mittagessen (-)	lunch
die Mitternacht	midnight
(ich) möchte	(I) would like
möchten Sie (möchtest du)	would you like
mögen (mag, mochte, hat gemocht)	to like
die Möhre (-n)	carrot
der Mokka	coffee (flavoured)
müde	tired
der Mülleimer (-)	dustbin
das Münster (-)	minster
die Münzentankstelle (-n)	coin operated petrol pump
die Münze (-n)	coin
das Museum (-een)	museum
der Musiker (-)	musician (masc.)
müssen (muß, mußte, hat gemußt)	to have to, must
die Mutter (¨)	mother
nach	after, to
nach Ihnen	after you
nachgießen (gießt . . . nach, goß . . . nach, hat nachgegossen)	to pour some more
nachmittags	in the afternoon
der/die/das nächste	the next
nächste Haltestelle	next stop (press button if you wish to alight)
die Nacht (¨e)	night
der Nachtisch (-e)	sweet, dessert
nachts	at night
nachzahlen, bitte	please insert more money
nahen	to sew
die Nähnadel (-n)	sewing needle
die Nahrungsmittel (pl.)	food
der Name (-n)	name
das Nasenbluten	nose bleed

die Nebellampe (-n)	fog lamp
nehmen (nimmt, nahm, hat genommen)	to take
neu	new
nicht	not
nichts	nothing
noch	still
Nordirland	Northern Ireland
Normal (Benzin)	three star petrol
der Notizblock (⁻e)	note pad
die Nummer (-n)	number
nur	only
nur Ausstieg	exit only
der Ober	waiter
oder	or
der Ohrring (-e)	earring
die Ohrenschmerzen (pl.)	ear-ache
das Öl (-e)	oil
der Öldruck	oil pressure
der Ölwechsel (-)	oil change
der Ort (-e)	place
das Paket (-e)	packet
die Paketannahme (-n)	counter for parcels (in post office)
der Paß (⁻sse)	passport
die Paßkontrolle (-n)	passport control
die Pension (-en)	guest house
der Personenzug (⁻e)	slow train
der Pfennig (-e)	Pfennig
das Pflaster	(sticky) plaster
das Pfund	pound
das Plastik (-s)	plastic
(einen) Platten haben	to have a flat tyre
der Platz (⁻e)	place, seat, square
die Platzreservierung (-en)	seat reservation
pleite (slang)	broke
die Polizei	police
die Polizeiwache (-n)	police station
die Pommes Frites (pl.)	chips
das Portemonnaie (-s)	purse
die Post	post office
die Postkarte (-n)	postcard
die Postwertzeichen (pl.)	postage stamps
der Preis (-e)	price
preiswert	good value for money
prima	great, wonderful

35

pro	per
prüfen	to check
der Pumpernickel	very dark rye bread
pünktlich	punctual(ly)
die Puppe (-n)	doll
der Quark	cottage cheese
das Radio (-s)	radio
die Raststätte (-n)	motorway restaurant
das Rathaus (¨er)	town hall
rauchen	to smoke
rechts	right
der Rechtsanwalt (¨e)	lawyer
der Regenmantel (¨)	raincoat
das R-Gespräch (-e)	collect call (reversed charge)
der Reifen (-)	tyre
die Reise (-n)	journey, trip
das Reisebüro (-s)	travel office
reisen	to travel
der Reisepaß (¨sse)	passport
der Reisescheck (-s)	traveller's cheque
die Reparatur (-en)	repair
der Rettich (-e)	long, white radish
der Rindsbraten (-)	beef joint
der Ring (-e)	ring
der Rosenkohl	Brussels sprouts
rot	red
der Rotwein	red wine
das Rückfahrtslicht (-er)	reversing light
die Rückenschmerzen (pl.)	backache
der Rückwärtsgang	reverse gear
ruhig	calm, quiet
der Saft (¨e)	juice
sagen	to say
die Sahne	cream
der Salat (-e)	salad
die Salbe (-n)	ointment
sauer	sour
die saure Gurke (-n)	gherkin
die S-Bahn (-en)	urban railway (above ground)
die Schallplatte (-n)	record
(eine) Schallplatte auflegen	to put on a record
der Schalthebel (-)	gear lever
die Schaltung	gears
schätzen	to estimate
der Scheibenwischer (-)	windscreen wiper

der Schein (-e)	banknote
der Scheinwerfer (-)	headlamp
der Schinken	ham
der Schirm (-e)	umbrella
die Schlachterei (-en)	butcher's shop
der Schlafsaal (¨e)	dormitory
schlecht	bad(ly)
schlechter	worse
schließen (schließt, schloß, hat geschlossen)	to close
das Schloß (¨er)	castle
der Schluck (¨e)	drop, gulp
der Schlüssel (-)	key
schmecken	to taste
schmeckt's?	do you like it (of food)
der Schmerz (-en)	pain
(sich) schneiden (schneidet, schnitt, hat geschnitten)	to cut (oneself)
schnell	fast
der Schnellbus (-se)	express bus
der Schnellimbiß (-sse)	snack bar
das Schnitzel (-)	fillet
der Schnupfen (-)	cold (in the nose)
die Schokolade (-n)	chocolate
der Schokoladekuchen (-)	chocolate cake
die Scholle (-n)	plaice
schön	nice, beautiful
der Schoppen (-)	2cl jug
Schottland	Scotland
schreiben (schreibt, schrieb, hat geschrieben)	to write
die Schreibwaren (pl.)	writing materials
schwarz	black
das Schwarzbrot (-e)	(loaf of) brown bread
die Schwarzwäldertorte (-n)	Black Forest gateau
der Schweinebraten (-)	pork joint, roast pork
die Schwellung (-en)	swelling
schwer zu sagen	difficult to say
die Schwester (-n)	sister
der Seemann (¨er)	sailor, seaman
sehr	very
die Seife (-n)	soap
seit	since
die Seite (-n)	side
die Sekretärin (-nen)	secretary (fem.)
die Selbstbedienung	self-service
sentimental	sentimental
separat	separate(ly)

37

servieren	to serve
sicher	sure, certain
der Sicherheitsgürtel (-)	safety belt
die Sicherheitsnadel (-n)	safety pin
das Siedfleisch	boiling beef
das Silber	silver
der Skizzierblock (¨e)	sketch pad (block)
das Sonderangebot (-e)	special offer
die Speisekarte (-n)	menu
der Speisesaal (¨e)	dining room
die Spezialität (-en)	speciality
das Spiel (-e)	game
der Spielplatz (¨e)	playground
die Spielwaren (pl.)	toys
der Spinat	spinach
die Sportanlage (-n)	sports centre
sprechen (spricht, sprach, hat gesprochen)	to speak
der Sprudel (-)	mineral water
die Stadtmitte (-n)	town centre
der Stadtplan (¨e)	town map
der Starter (-)	starter
das Steak (-s)	steak
die Steckdose (-n)	wall plug, point
stehen (steht, stand, hat gestanden)	to stand
stehlen (stiehlt, stahl hat gestohlen)	to steal
das Steuerrad (¨er)	steering wheel
die Steuerung	steering
stören	to disturb
stört es Sie?	do you mind?
die Straße (-n)	street
die Straßenbahn (-en)	tram
die Straßenkarte (-n)	road map
das Stück (-e)	piece, a bit, silver coin
die Stunde (-n)	hour
stürmisch	stormy, rough
Super (Benzin)	four star petrol
der Supermarkt (¨e)	supermarket
der Tag (-e)	day
die Tagessuppe (-n)	soup of the day
täglich	daily
die Tankstelle (-n)	petrol station
der Tankwart (¨e)	petrol pump attendant
das Taschentuch (¨er)	handkerchief
die Tasse (-n)	cup

das Taxi (-s)	taxi
der TE	trans-Europa Express
der Tee	tea
das Telegramm (-e)	telegram
der Termin (-e)	appointment
einen Termin vereinbaren	to make an appointment
teuer	expensive
das Theater (-)	theatre
der Tiergarten (˝)	zoo
die Tinte (-n)	ink
der Tisch (-e)	table
den Tisch decken	to lay the table
den Tisch abräumen	to clear the table
die Toilette (-n)	toilet
die Tomate (-n)	tomato
trinken (trinkt, trank, hat getrunken)	to drink
tschüß	cheerio, ta-ta
die U-Bahn (-en)	underground train
die Überfahrt (-en)	(sea) crossing
das Übergewicht	excess weight
die Übernachtung (-en)	night-stay
überqueren	to cross (a road)
übersetzen	to translate
der Umbau	renovation
der Umschlag (˝e)	envelope
umsteigen (steigt . . . um, stieg . . . um, ist umgestiegen)	to change (trains)
um wieviel Uhr	at what time
ungefähr	about, approximately
das Unternehmen (-)	business
unterschreiben (unterschreibt, unterschrieb, hat unterschrieben)	to sign
unterwegs	on the way, travelling
die Vanille	vanilla
der Vater (˝)	father
der Ventilator (-en)	fan (in a car)
der Ventilatorriemen (-)	fan belt
der Verbandstoff	dressing (medical)
verboten	forbidden, not allowed
die Verdauungsbeschwerden (pl.)	indigestion
der Vergaser (-)	carburettor
die Verkäuferin (-nen)	sales assistant (fem.)

verlieren (verliert, verlor, hat verloren)	to lose
vermieten	to let
die Verspätung (-en)	delay
Verspätung haben	to be late
verstauchen	to sprain
verstehen (versteht, verstand, hat verstanden)	to understand
die Verstopfung	constipation
versuchen	to try
der Verteiler (-)	distributor
der Vertreter (-)	rep, representative
der Verwalter (-)	administrator, manager
die Verwaltung (-en)	administration
verweigern	to refuse
Verzeihung	pardon (me), I beg your pardon
verzollen	to declare (at Customs)
viel	much
viel Vergnügen, viel Spaß	have fun
viele	many
vielen Dank	many thanks, thanks a lot
viermal	four times, for four
voll	full
vollautomatisch	fully automatic
die Vollpension (-en)	full board (in a hotel)
vorbeikommen (kommt . . . vorbei, kam . . . vorbei, ist vorbeigekommen)	to call on someone
das Vorderrad (¨er)	front wheel
vorgestern	the day before yesterday
vormittags	in the morning
der Vorname (-n)	Christian name, first name
vorn einsteigen	enter in front
der Wagen (-)	car, vehicle
der Wagenheber (-)	jack
wann	when
war	was
der Warteraum (¨e)	waiting room
was	what
was für	what kind
was ist denn los	what's the matter
(sich) waschen, wäscht, wusch, hat gewaschen)	to wash (oneself)
der Waschlappen (-)	flannel
das Waschpulver (-)	washing powder
die Waschstraße (-n)	car wash (automatic)

40

das Wasser (-)	water
die Wasserpumpe (-n)	water pump
der Wechsel	change (counter for changing currency in a bank)
wechseln	to change
die Wechselstube (-n)	office for changing currency
wegen	because of
wehtun (tut . . . weh, tat . . . weh, hat wehgetan)	to hurt
weich gesotten	soft boiled
der Wein (-e)	wine
die Weinkarte (-n)	wine list
die Weinstube (-n)	wine bar
weiß	white
das Weißbrot (-e)	white bread
der Weißwein (-e)	white wine
weit	far
welcher (e, es)	which
wenig	little, not much
wenn	when, if
werden (wird, wurde, ist geworden)	to become
der Wert (-e)	value
wertvoll	valuable
wie	how
wie lange	how long
wie geht es Ihnen, (dir)	how are you
wieder	again
wiederholen	to repeat
wiedersehen (sieht . . . wieder, sah . . . wieder, hat wiedergesehen)	to see again
wie steht der Kurs	what is the rate of exchange
wieviel	how much
wieviel darf es kosten	what price category were you thinking of
wieviele	how many
willkommen	welcome
die Windjacke	anorak
die Windschutzscheibe (-n)	windscreen
wo	where
wo fehlt's denn	what's wrong
die Woche (-n)	week
woher	from where, where from
wohnen	to live
der Wohnwagen (-)	caravan
das Wörterbuch (¨er)	dictionary
würden Sie (würdest du)	would you

41

die Wurst (̈e)	sausage
die Wurstwaren (pl.)	sausages
die Wurzel (-n)	carrot, root
zahlen	to pay
der Zahnarzt (̈e)	dentist
die Zahnpasta (-en)	toothpaste
die Zahnschmerzen (pl.)	tooth-ache
zeigen	to show
die Zeitung (-en)	newspaper
die Zeitschrift (-en)	magazine
das Zelt (-e)	tent
ziehen (zieht, zog, hat gezogen)	to pull
das Zimmer (-)	room
der Zimmernachweis ⎫	accommodation
die Zimmervermittlung ⎭	bureau
der Zoll	Customs
zu	to, too
der Zug (̈e)	train
die Zündkerze (-n)	spark plug
die Zündung	ignition
zurück	back
zurücktreten, bitte	step back, please
zusammen	together
der Zutritt	admission
zweimal	twice, for two
zweimal Köln	two tickets to Cologne
der/die/das zweite	the second
zweite Klasse	second class
der Zwieback (-e)	rusk
der Zwirn (-e)	cotton, thread
zwischen	between

about, approximately	etwa, ungefähr
to accept	annehmen
accommodation bureau	der Zimmernachweis, die Zimmervermittlung
address	die Anschrift
administration	die Verwaltung
administrator	der Verwalter
admission	der Zutritt
aerogramme	der Luftpostbrief
to afford	(sich) leisten
after, to	nach
after you	nach Ihnen/dir
again	wieder
airport	der Flughafen
air ticket	die Flugkarte
allergic	allergisch
all together	alles zusammen
all right if it's a bit over	darf's etwas mehr sein
announcement	die Bekanntmachung
another drop	noch ein Schluck
anorak	die Windjacke
anti-freeze	der Frostschutz
anything else	darf's sonst noch was sein
apple juice	der Apfelsaft
apple strudel	der Apfelstrudel
appointment	der Termin
to arrive	ankommen
arrival	die Ankunft
article, item	der Artikel
artist	der Künstler, die Künstlerin
as from	ab
as far as, until	bis
ashtray	der Aschenbecher
aspirin	das Aspirin
at	bei
at what time	um wieviel Uhr
automatic	automatisch
backache	Rückenschmerzen (pl.)
back wheel	das Hinterrad
bacon	der Frühstücksspeck
bad	schlecht
bakery	die Bäckerei
ball point pen	der Kugelschreiber
bank	die Bank

43

bath	das Bad
to bathe	baden
bathroom	das Badezimmer
bathtowel	das Badtuch
battery	die Batterie
bean	die Bohne
bedroom	das Schlafzimmer
bed	das Bett
beef joint	der Schweinebraten
beer	das Bier
before	vor
better	besser
between	zwischen
bill	die Rechnung
(the) bill, please	zahlen, bitte
biscuit	der Keks
black	schwarz
Black Forest gateau	der Schwarzwälderkuchen
blue	blau
board	die Tafel
boats for hire	Boote zu vermieten
boiling beef	das Siedfleisch
to book	buchen
bookshop	der Buchladen, die Buchhandlung
booth	die Zelle, die Kabine
bottle	die Flasche
boy	der Junge
bracelet	das Armband
brake	die Bremse
brakelight	das Bremslicht
bread	das Brot
breakdown service	die Autohilfe
breakfast	das Frühstück
British	britisch
broke	pleite
brothers and sisters	Geschwister (pl.)
brother	der Bruder
brown bread	das Schwarzbrot
brown	braun
brush	die Bürste
Brussels sprouts	der Rosenkohl
(light) bulb	die Birne
businessman	der Kaufmann, der Geschäftsmann
butcher's shop	die Fleischerei, die Schlachterei, die Metzgerei
to buy	kaufen

café	das Café
to call	rufen, anrufen
to be called	heißen
calm	ruhig
camping site	der Campingplatz
camping stove	der Campingofen
car	das Auto, der Wagen
caravan	der Wohnwagen
car accessories	der Autozubehör
carburettor	der Vergaser
car registration	die Autonummer
carrot	die Wurzel, die Möhre
to cash	einlösen, kassieren
cashier	die Kassiererin
castle	das Schloß
cathedral	die Kathedrale, der Dom
Catholic	katholisch
cauliflower	der Blumenkohl
change	der Wechsel, die Wechselstube
to change	umwechseln, wechseln
charcoal	die Holzkohle
charge	die Gebühr
to (re)charge	aufladen
cheap	billig
to check	prüfen
check-in	die Abfertigung
cheerio, ta-ta	tschüß
cheese	der Käse
cheesecake	der Käsekuchen
chemist's shop	die Apotheke
cherry-brandy gateau	die Kirschtorte
chicken	das Hähnchen
chips	Pommes Frites (pl.)
chocolate cake	der Schokoladekuchen
chocolate	die Schokolade
Christian name	der Vorname
church	die Kirche
cinema	das Kino
civil servant	der Beamte
to clear the table	den Tisch abräumen
clerk	der Büroangestellte
to close	schließen
closed for renovation	wegen Umbau geschlossen
clutch	die Kupplung
cocoa	der Kakao
cod	der Kabeljau
coffee	der Kaffee
coin	die Münze

45

Coke (Coca Cola)	die Kola
colour film	der Farbfilm
collect call	das R-Gespräch
comb	der Kamm
confectioner's	die Konditorei
to confirm	bestätigen
connection	der Anschluß, die Verbindung
consommé, clear soup	die klare Brühe
constipation	die Verstopfung
cottage cheese	der Quark
cotton (thread)	der Zwirn
cough	der Husten
cough-sweet	das Hustenbonbon
could you	könnten Sie (könntest du)
cream	die Sahne
croquette potatoes	der Kartoffelpuffer
to cross	überqueren
cucumber	die Gurke
cup	die Tasse
Customs	der Zoll
to cut (oneself)	(sich) schneiden
daily	täglich
day	der Tag
day before yesterday	vorgestern
to declare (at Customs)	verzollen
delay	die Verspätung
Denmark	Dänemark
dentist	der Zahnarzt
departure	die Abfahrt, der Abflug
to describe	beschreiben
dessert	der Nachtisch
diarrhoea	der Durchfall
dictionary	das Wörterbuch
difficult	schwer, schwierig
difficult to say	schwer zu sagen
dining room	der Speisesaal
dinner	das Abendessen, das Abendbrot
discotheque	die Diskothek
disinfectant	das Desinfektionsmittel
distilled	destilliert
distributor	der Verteiler
do you mind	stört es Sie (dich)
docks	der Hafen
domestic flight	der Inland-Flug
don't mention it	bitte schön, bitte sehr
dormitory	der Schlafsaal

double room	das Doppelzimmer
dressing	der Verbandstoff
drink	das Getränk
to drink	trinken
to dry	trocknen, abtrocknen
dustbin	der Mülleimer
ear-ache	Ohrenschmerzen (pl.)
earring	der Ohrring
to eat	essen
egg	das Ei
engineer	der Ingenieur
England	England
English	englisch
enough	genug
to enquire	nachfragen, sich erkundigen
enter at the front/back	vorn/hinten einsteigen
envelope	der Umschlag
Europa	Europe
European and overseas flight	der Ausland-Flug
evening	der Abend
everything	alles
excess weight	das Übergewicht
to excuse	(sich) entschuldigen
exit only	nur Ausstieg
to expect	erwarten
express letter	der Eilbrief
express bus	der Schnellbus
factory worker	der Fabrikarbeiter
fan belt	der Treibriemen
far	weit
farmer	der Landwirt
father	der Vater
to feel	(sich) fühlen
(I) feel fine	es geht mir gut
ferry	die Fähre
few	einige
to fill up	auftanken
to fill in	ausfüllen, (sich) eintragen
fillet	das Schnitzel
film	der Film
to find	finden
first	erste (r)
flannel	der Waschlappen
flat battery	die leere Batterie
(to have a) flat tyre	(einen) Platten (haben)
flight	der Flug

florist's	das Blumengeschäft
'flu	die Grippe
foglamp	die Nebellampe
foot	der Fuß
footbrake	die Fußbremse
on foot	zu Fuß
for	für
French	französisch
fresh	frisch
freshly made today	heute ganz frisch
from	von, aus
front wheel	das Vorderrad
frying sausage	die Bratwurst
fuel pump	die Benzinpumpe
full	voll
(have) fun	viel Vergnügen, viel Spaß
game	das Spiel
gear	der Gang
gearbox	das Getriebe
gear lever	der Schalthebel
gents	Herren (pl.)
get well soon	gute Besserung
German	deutsch
gherkin	die saure Gurke
girl friend	die Freundin
to give	geben
gladly	gerne
glass	das Glas
glove	der Handschuh
to go	gehen
go ahead (on telephone)	bitte sprechen
go to the trouble	sich Mühe machen
gold	das Gold
good	gut
good day	guten Tag
good evening	guten Abend
good morning	guten Morgen
good night	gute Nacht
good bye (see you again etc.)	auf Wiedersehen
good value for money	preiswert
gramme	das Gramm
green	grün
hair	das Haar
hairbrush	die Haarbürste
hairdryer	der Haartrockner, der Föhn
half a litre	halber Liter

ham	der Schinken
hand	die Hand
handbag	die Handtasche
handbrake	die Handbremse
handkerchief	das Taschentuch
hand luggage	das Handgepäck
hangover	der Kater
Hanover	Hannover
harbour	der Hafen
harbour circuit	die Hafenrundfahrt
hard-boiled	hart gesotten
hat	der Hut
hayfever	der Heuschnupfen
headache	Kopfschmerzen (pl.)
headlamp (of cars)	die Lampe
headlight	der Scheinwerfer
hearty	herzlich
heating	die Heizung
to help	helfen
here	hier
high	hoch
home (at)	zu Hause
honey	der Honig
to hope	hoffen
horn	die Hupe
hospital	das Krankenhaus
hostel	die Herberge
hotel full	Hotel besetzt
hotel guide	der Hotelnachweis, die Hotelvermittlung
hour	die Stunde
hours of business	Geschäftszeiten (pl.)
housewife	die Hausfrau
how	wie
how long	wie lang
how many	wieviele
how much	wieviel
how much do you think it's worth	wie hoch schätzen Sie den Wert
hungry	hungrig
to hurt	wehtun
I	ich
I am broke	ich bin pleite
I am called . . .	ich heiße . . .
I can't afford that	das kann ich mir nicht leisten
I don't understand	ich verstehe nicht
I must	ich muß

49

I should like	ich möchte
ice cream	das Eis
ice rink	die Kunsteisbahn
if	wenn
ignition	die Zündung
to include	(mit)einschließen
included	inbegriffen
inclusive	inklusiv
indicator	das Blinklicht
indigestion	die Verdauungsstörung
indoor swimming pool	das Hallenbad
information	die Auskunft
ink	die Tinte
inn	der Gasthof
invalids	Behinderte (pl.)
Ireland	Irland
iron	das Bügeleisen
to iron	bügeln
is there	gibt es
it	es
item	der Artikel
jack	der Wagenheber
jacket	die Jacke
joint	der Braten
(2cl) jug	der Schoppen
junction	die Kreuzung
just	gleich, eben
just round the corner	gleich um die Ecke
key	der Schlüssel
kilo	das Kilo
kind	liebenswürdig, freundlich
kiosk	der Kiosk
kitchen	die Küche
laboratory assistant	der Laborant, die Laborantin
lamb chop	das Hammelkotelett
lamb joint	der Hammelbraten
to land	landen
late	spät, verspätet
lawyer	der Rechtsanwalt
to lay (the table)	den Tisch decken
(at) least	mindestens
leather	das Leder
to leave	abfahren, verlassen
left	links
(on) left hand side	auf der linken Seite

left luggage	die Gepäckaufbewährung
less	weniger
letter	der Brief
letter box	der Briefkasten
lever	der Hebel
lift	der Fahrstuhl
lightswitch	der Lichtschalter
to like	mögen, gerne haben
litre	der Liter
little	wenig, klein
a little something	eine Kleinigkeit
to live	wohnen, leben
long	lang
lorry driver	der Lastfahrer
to lose	verlieren
lost property office	das Fundbüro
(a) lot	viel
lounge	der Aufenthaltsraum, das Wohnzimmer
lunch	das Mittagessen
magazine	die Zeitschrift
main station	der Hauptbahnhof
make	die Marke
to make an appointment	einen Termin vereinbaren
many	viele
map	die Karte
Mark (currency)	die Mark
Mark coin	die Markmünze
market square	der Marktplatz
mashed potatoes	der Kartoffelbrei
may I	darf ich
meal	die Mahlzeit
to mean	bedeuten
meat	Fleischwaren (pl.)
meat ball	die Frikadelle
mechanic	der Mechaniker
medical assistant	der Arztgehilfe, die Arztgehilfin
to meet	kennenlernen, treffen
membership card	die Mitgliedskarte
menu	das Menu
metre	der Meter
midnight	die Mitternacht
minced meat	das Hackfleisch
miner	der Bergmann
mineral water	der Sprudel, das Mineralwasser

51

minster	das Münster
minute	die Minute
Miss	das Fräulein
money	das Geld
more	mehr
morning	der Morgen
mother	die Mutter
motorway restaurant	die Raststätte
Munich	München
museum	das Museum
musician	der Musiker
name	der Name
near	in der Nähe
near a kiosk	bei einem Kiosk
necklace	die Halskette
to need	brauchen
new	neu
newspaper	die Zeitung
(the) next	der/die/das nächste
next stop (press button to alight)	die nächste Haltestelle
night	die Nacht
(at) night	nachts
no, not a	kein, keine
no admission without valid ticket	Einstieg nur mit gültigem Fahrschein
no liability accepted for hats, coats, etc.	für Garderobe wird nicht gehaftet
Northern Ireland	Nordirland
nose bleed	das Nasenbluten
not	nicht
not too bad	es geht
(bank) note	der Schein
note pad	der Notizblock
nothing	nichts
now	jetzt
number	die Nummer
Nuremberg	Nürnberg
nurse	die Krankenschwester
nursery teacher	die Kindergärtnerin
occupation (job)	der Beruf, die Beschäftigung
office	das Büro
office hours	Bürozeiten (pl.)
oil	das Öl
oil change	der Ölwechsel
oil pressure	der Öldruck

ointment	die Salbe
okay	in Ordnung
old	alt
on	auf
one	eins
one ticket to Munich	einmal München
only	nur
only child	das Einzelkind
to open	öffnen
open	geöffnet
open air swimming pool	das Freibad
or	oder
out of order	außer Betrieb
over	über, drüber
own	eigen
packet	das Paket
pain	der Schmerz
pardon	Verzeihung
parents	Eltern (pl.)
passport	der Paß, der Reisepaß
passport control	die Paßkontrolle
to pay	zahlen
paying-out counter	die Kasse
pea	die Erbse
pedestrian crossing	der Fußgängerstreifen
pendant	die Halskette
per	pro
petrol	das Benzin
petrol pump attendant	der Tankwart
petrol station	die Tankstelle
Pfennig	der Pfennig
picture postcard	die Ansichtskarte
piece	das Stück
place	der Platz
plaice	die Scholle
plastic	das Plastik
platform	das Gleis
platform ticket	die Bahnsteigkarte
playground	der Spielplatz
please	bitte
please insert more money	nachzahlen, bitte
point, wall plug	die Steckdose
police	die Polizei
police station	die Polizeiwache
pork chop	das Schweinekotelett
pork joint	der Schweinebraten
port	der Hafen

porter	der Gepäckträger
postage stamps	Postwertzeichen (pl.)
postcard	die Postkarte
post office	die Post
pound	das Pfund
to pour	gießen, nachgießen
present	das Geschenk
press here (for doors to open)	hier drücken
pressure	der Druck
price	der Preis
Protestant	evangelisch
punctual	pünktlich
purse	das Portemonnaie
to push	schieben, anschieben, stoßen
radiator (of cars)	der Kühler
radio	das Radio
radish	der Rettich
railway employee	der Bahnangestellter
raincoat	der Regenmantel
rash (of skin)	der Ausschlag
rate of exchange	der Kurs
rather	lieber
rear light	die Hecklampe
record	die Schallplatte
reception	der Empfang
red	rot
red wine	der Rotwein
to refuse	verweigern
to register	(sich) eintragen
registered letter	der Einschreibebrief
renovation	der Umbau
repair	die Reparatur
to repeat	wiederholen
representative (rep)	der Vertreter
to request	bitten
requested	ist gebeten
reservation	die Reservierung
restaurant	die Gaststätte, das Gasthaus
rest chair	der Liegeplatz
return (ticket)	hin und zurück
reverse gear	der Rückwärtsgang
reversing light	das Rückfahrtslicht
reversed charge call	das R-Gespräch
right (direction)	rechts
right	richtig
to ring (bell)	klingeln
to ring (phone)	anrufen

road map	die Straßenkarte
roast pork	der Schweinebraten
roll (bread)	das Brötchen
room	das Zimmer
rough (sea)	stürmisch, bewegt
round the corner	um die Ecke
rusk	der Zwieback
safety belt	der Sicherheitsgürtel
safety pin	die Sicherheitsnadel
sailor	der Seemann
salad	der Salat
Salami-type sausage	die Mettwurst
sales assistant	die Verkäuferin (fem.)
	der Verkäufer (masc,)
sanitary towel	die Damenbinde
sausage	die Wurst
to say	sagen
scissors	die Schere
Scotland	Schottland
seat reservation	die Platzreservierung
the second	der/die/das zweite
secretary	die Sekretärin (fem.)
	der Sekretär (masc.)
to see	sehen
selection	die Auswahl
self-employed	selbständiger Unternehmer
self service	die Selbstbedienung
sentimental	sentimental
separate(ly)	separat
to serve	bedienen
service	die Bedienung
to sew	nähen
sewing needle	die Nähnadel
shopping centre	das Einkaufszentrum
short, thick sausage	die Knackwurst, der Cervelat
to show	zeigen
shower	die Dusche
to shower, take a shower	duschen
sick (to feel)	übel
side	die Seite
to sign	unterschreiben
silver	das Silber
since	seit
single (ticket)	einfach
single room	das Einzelzimmer
sister	die Schwester
sketchblock	der Skizzierblock

sliced cold meat	der Aufschnitt
slot for inserting ticket	die Fahrkartenentwertung
slow	langsam
slow train	der Personenzug
sluggish, doesn't pull	zieht nicht
small change	das Kleingeld
to smoke	rauchen
snack bar	der Schnellimbiß
soap	die Seife
social worker	die Fürsorgerin, der Fürsorger
soft-boiled	weich gesotten
some	einige
something	etwas
something is wrong with my car	mit meinem Wagen ist etwas nicht in Ordnung
soon	bald
soup of the day	die Tagessuppe
sour	sauer
souvenir	das Andenken
spare wheel	das Ersatzrad
spare tyre	der Ersatzreifen
spark plug	die Zündkerze
to speak	sprechen
special offer	das Sonderangebot
speciality	die Spezialität
to spell	buchstabieren
spinach	der Spinat
sports centre	die Sportanlage
to sprain (a limb)	verstauchen
stamp (postage)	die Marke, die Briefmarke
to stand	stehen
three star (petrol)	Normal
four star (petrol)	Super
to start	starten, anspringen
starter	der Starter
station	der Bahnhof
steak	das Steak
steering	die Steuerung
steering wheel	das Steuerrad
step back, please	zurücktreten, bitte
stewing beef	das Siedfleisch
sticky plaster	das Pflaster, das Heftpflaster
stomach-ache	Magenschmerzen (pl.)
stormy (sea)	stürmisch
straight ahead	geradeaus
strawberry gateau	die Erdbeertorte
street	die Straße
subway	die Unterführung

suitcase	der Koffer
supermarket	der Supermarkt
sure	sicher
surname	der Familienname
Swedish type crisp bread	das Knäckebrot
sweet (dessert)	der Nachtisch
swelling	die Schwellung
swollen	geschwollen
table	der Tisch
to take	nehmen
to taste	schmecken, versuchen
tasty	lecker
taxi	das Taxi
tea	der Tee
teacher	der Lehrer, die Lehrerin
telegram	das Telegramm
telephone	der Fernsprecher
telephone call	das Ferngespräch
temperature (of body)	das Fieber
tent	das Zelt
thanks	danke, ich bedanke mich
thank you very much	danke schön
thanks a lot	vielen Dank
that	das
that's all	das ist alles
that's right	ganz richtig
theatre	das Theater
then	dann
there	da, dort
thermometer	der Fiebermesser
to think	glauben, denken
thirsty	durstig
this	dieser (e, es)
this morning/afternoon	heute morgen/nachmittag
ticket	die Fahrkarte
ticket machine	der Fahrkartenautomat
tired	müde
to	nach, zu
to the trains	zu den Zügen
together	zusammen
toilet	die Toilette
tomato	die Tomate
too expensive	zu teuer
too fast	zu schnell
tooth-ache	Zahnschmerzen (pl.)
toothpaste	die Zahnpasta
to tow	(ab) schleppen

town centre	die Stadtmitte
town hall	das Rathaus
town map	der Stadtplan
toy	das Spielzeug
traffic light	die Ampel, die Verkehrsampel
train	der Zug, die Eisenbahn
tram	die Straßenbahn
trans-Europa express	der TE
to translate	übersetzen
to travel	reisen
traveller's cheque	der Reisescheck
travel office	das Reisebüro
trip	die Reise
trouble	die Mühe
to try	versuchen
two tickets to Cologne	zweimal Köln
to turn	abbiegen, drehen
underground train	die U-Bahn
to understand	verstehen
unfortunately	leider
until	bis
urban railway	die S-Bahn
vacancy (rooms)	Zimmer frei
value	der Wert
valuable	wertvoll
vanilla	die Vanille
V.A.T.	die Mehrwertsteuer
Viennese bread	der Eierzopf
waiter	der Ober
waiting room	der Warteraum, der Wartesaal
Wales	Wales, Wallisien
wallet	die Brieftasche
wall plug	die Steckdose
was	war
to wash	waschen
to wash up (dishes)	das Geschirr spülen
washing powder	das Waschpulver
washroom	der Waschraum
to watch television	fernsehen
water	das Wasser
water pump	die Wasserpumpe
weight	das Gewicht
welcome	willkommen
what	was
what are you called	wie heißen Sie (heißt du)

what do you call this in German	wie heißt das auf Deutsch
what does it mean	was bedeutet das
what make	welche Marke
what's the matter	was ist denn los
what price category were you thinking of	wieviel darf's kosten
what's wrong	wo fehlt's denn
when	wann, wenn
where	wo
where from	von wo
which	welche, welcher
white	weiß
white bread	das Weißbrot
white wine	der Weißwein
whole	ganz
windscreen	die Windschutzscheibe
windscreen wiper	der Scheibenwischer
wine	der Wein
wine list	die Weinkarte
wine bar	die Weinstube
with	mit
to work	arbeiten
worth	wert
would you	würden Sie (würdest du)
wrist-watch	die Armbanduhr
to write	schreiben
writing pad	das Briefpapier
writing materials	Schreibwaren (pl.)
wrong	falsch
yellow	gelb
yes	ja
yesterday	gestern
yesterday evening	gestern abend
you're welcome	bitte schön, bitte sehr
zoo	der Tiergarten